CHURCH

A Bible Study Wordbook for Kids

by Richard E. Todd

This Wordbook Belongs To . . .

WingSpread Publishers
Camp Hill, Pennsylvania

Message to Parents/ Teachers

In order for this Bible study wordbook to be profitable for your children, your help is needed. Try to be available to answer questions that might arise, but please, as much as possible, allow your children to discover these important Bible truths for themselves.

Instructions for Parents/Teachers

1. This Bible study wordbook entitled *Church* addresses the issues of commitment to and involvement in your local church. Another adult can work with the student when a parent cannot participate in the study. This wordbook is part of a series that is most beneficial when used together. Other wordbooks in this series include *Salvation, Baptism, Communion* and *Giving*.

2. Allow your student to study the material on his/her own as much as possible. Children in early elementary grades might need assistance in completing some sections of the wordbook.

3. You should grade the fill-in sections and the final quiz. Review the answers and be sure your student understands the issues involved. The quiz answers are on page 3.

4. The fifth chapter in this wordbook entitled "How Do I Join My Church?" concerns local church membership. Each church has different requirements. Talk with your pastor if your student has questions about joining your local church.

5. The student completing this wordbook is asked in chapter 2 to list three things that he/she enjoys doing at church. If the student expresses negative responses concerning his/her church experiences, set a goal right away to encourage and develop positive ones.

6. In chapter 4, the student is asked if he/she is part of God's family. Please look at the response and discuss if needed.

7. Purchase a box of thank-you notes and send special greetings to one or more people in your church who minister to your family on a regular basis. This might be the pastor, music director, Sunday school teacher, usher or others.

8. Baptism is a testimony to the presence of Christ in a believer's life. This is mentioned to the student in chapter 4. The *Baptism* wordbook is available for further study by the student.

9. Different activities are used in worship services by different churches (even within the same denominations). During an upcoming vacation, your family might benefit richly by attending a worship service at another church in the area where you are traveling.

10. The topics in each chapter have been organized so that a parent or a teacher can teach them in several sessions.

QUIZ ANSWERS (PAGES 27–28):

GOOD REASON, WRONG REASON: 1. wrong, wrong, good, wrong, good **2.** sing, praise, pray, etc. **3.** learn, do **TRUE/FALSE: 1.** T **2.** F **3.** T **4.** F **5.** T **6.** T **7.** T **8.** F

Pastor Richard E. Todd is Senior Pastor of Community Grace Brethren Church in Whittier, California. He first joined the staff there in 1982 as Associate Pastor and became Senior Pastor in 1987. He and his wife, Claudia, have three sons: Ryan, Riley and Rory.

CHURCH

WingSpread Publishers

Camp Hill, Pennsylvania
www.wingspreadpublishers.com

1-800-884-4571
A division of Zur Ltd.

Church: A Bible Study Wordbook for Kids
by Richard E. Todd
ISBN: 978-1-60066-196-9
©1988, 2008 by Richard E. Todd

12   5 4 3 2

Cover illustrations by Rick Hemphill
Interior design by Pam Fogle

Originally published by Crosswalk Resources

WHAT iS A CHURCH LiKE?

CHURCHES CAN LOOK DiFFERENT.

"We who believe are carefully joined together with Christ as parts of a beautiful, constantly growing temple for God. And you also are joined with him and with each other by the Spirit, and are part of this dwelling place of God." Ephesians 2:21–22, TLB

Some churches look like this.

Other churches look like stores or offices.

LOOK CLOSELY AT THESE TWO PICTURES. WHAT DO YOU SEE THAT iS DiFFERENT ABOUT THEM?

WHaT DoeS YoUR CHURCH LooK LiKe?

Draw a picture of your church building in the space below. You may also cut a picture from a magazine or a newspaper that looks like your church and paste it in this box. Write the name of your church at the top when you start.

A CHURCH IS MORE THAN A BUILDING.

A church is a group of people who are members of God's family and meet together to **learn** and **do** what pleases Him. Only people make a church. All kinds of people make a church: boys, girls, moms, dads, brothers, sisters, aunts, uncles, grandmas and grandpas.

SOMETIMES THE BUILDING IS CALLED THE CHURCH.

BUT THE SPECIAL THING THAT MAKES IT A CHURCH IS THE "P _ _ _ _ _ ."

(Fill in each blank with a letter to complete the sentence.)

 Jesus said, "I will build my church." Matthew 16:18

Jesus is doing what He said He would do . . . building strong churches. Remember that the church is people, so Jesus is helping people to know Him . . . people in churches everywhere.

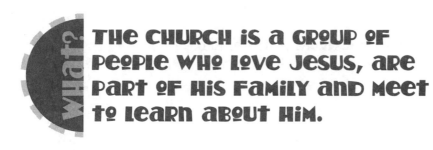

THE CHURCH IS A GROUP OF PEOPLE WHO LOVE JESUS, ARE PART OF HIS FAMILY AND MEET TO LEARN ABOUT HIM.

WHO ARE SOME OF THE PEOPLE IN YOUR CHURCH?

If you don't know their names, ask them on Sunday.

A CHILD YOUNGER THAN YOU: _____

A CHILD OLDER THAN YOU: _____

SOMEONE WITH A BABY: _____

A TEENAGER: _____

AN OLDER ADULT: _____

THESE PEOPLE ALL MAKE UP THE CHURCH!

WHaT Does a CHURCH Look Like?

Draw a picture of your church. Do not draw a picture of the building, but draw the people you listed. Be sure to include yourself.

WHAT HAPPENS at CHURCH?

what? PEOPLE GO TO CHURCH FOR MANY REASONS.

Some people go to church to make friends with others who love Jesus.

Some people attend church to sing songs about Jesus, listen to Bible stories and do fun things.

Some people go to church every Sunday with everyone from their family.

I GO TO CHURCH BECAUSE _____

_____

The Bible says the friends of Jesus enjoy being at church.

 "I was happy when they said to me, 'Let's go to the Temple of the Lord.'" Psalm 122:1

 "The believers met together" and were "happy to share their food. . . . They praised God, and all the people liked them." Acts 2:46–47

place a CHECK BY the activities that YOU Have DONE at YOUR CHURCH at least once:

 ATTENDED VACATION BIBLE SCHOOL.

 CELEBRATED COMMUNION.

 Went to CAMP (overnight, weekend or week-long).

 ATTENDED SUNDAY SCHOOL.

 HELPED at a CLEANUP OR WORKDAY.

 SANG in a CHOIR.

 Watched a BIBLE STORY VIDEO.

 RODE YOUR CHURCH BUS to an activity.

 YOUR Family HAD DINNER With another Family FROM CHURCH.

CROSSWORD PUZZLE

ACROSS

1 When you bring a friend to church, he/she is called a _____.

4 The day of the week that most people go to church.

5 When you become a member, you _____ the church.

6 When there is an offering at church, people _____ money.

Down

2 The Book God wants people to teach in church.

3 One step in learning the Bible is to _____ it.

4 People sitting in the congregation _____ songs during a church service.

7 When you ask God to help people, you _____ for them.

GOING to CHURCH Maze

HELP BILLY FIND HIS WAY to CHURCH.

Start Here

Puzzle created by *Puzzlemaker* from Discovery Channel School. Used by permission.

COLORING PAGE

A CHURCH iS a GROUP OF PEOPLE WHO ARE MEMBERS OF GOD'S FAMILY AND MEET TOGETHER TO LEARN AND DO WHAT PLEASES HIM.

We can learn what Jesus wants us to do at church—by reading what the Bible says Jesus did while He was here on earth. We can also learn what the followers of Jesus did at church by reading the Bible. The Bible verses below talk about the different things Jesus and His followers taught and did.

CAN YOU FIND AT LEAST THREE THINGS THEY TAUGHT AND DID? WRITE THEM AT THE BOTTOM OF THE NEXT PAGE.

 Sing "psalms, hymns, and spiritual songs."
Ephesians 5:19

 "All the people were praising God for what had been done." Acts 4:21–22

 Jesus said, "You will receive power. You will be my witnesses—in Jerusalem, in all of Judea, in Samaria, and in every part of the world." Acts 1:8

 "Christ gave each one of us a special gift. Each one received what Christ wanted to give him. Christ gave those gifts to prepare God's holy people for the work of serving." Ephesians 4:7, 12

"Then Jesus began to explain everything that had been written about himself in the Scriptures." Luke 24:27

 "The apostles were telling people that the Lord Jesus was truly raised from death. And God blessed all the believers very much." Acts 4:33

 "You should not stay away from the church meetings, as some are doing. But you should meet together and encourage each other." Hebrews 10:25

 "When a good man prays, great things happen." James 5:16

 "We can comfort others when they have trouble . . . with the same comfort that God gives us." 2 Corinthians 1:4

 "They spent their time learning the apostles' teaching. They continued to share . . . to pray together . . . and gave . . . to those people who needed it. The believers met together in the Temple." Acts 2:42, 45–46

WRITE DOWN THREE THINGS JESUS AND HIS FOLLOWERS TAUGHT ABOUT CHURCH:

1. _____

2. _____

3. _____

I enjoy Doing these things at Church:

One thing I enjoy doing at my church is _____

_____

Another thing I enjoy doing at my church is _____

_____

A third thing I enjoy doing at my church is _____

If you need help answering these questions, read the message in the box below.

Here are some ideas for you:

1. Do you like singing songs about Jesus?
2. Do you like listening to Bible stories?
3. Is there something special you do every week at church to help?
4. Is there a teacher or other adult at church whom you would like to help with the job they do at church? Talk with your parents about asking that adult if you can help.

If you haven't chosen three things you like to do at church, ask several people at your church what they like to do.

WHAT DOES it MEAN to BE in THE CHURCH?

BEiNG a MEMBER OF tHE CHURCH MEaNS tHat PEOPLE WiLL BE COUNtiNG ON YOU!

There are special things that Jesus will help you do at your church. As you attend regularly, you will find out what those special things are. You will enjoy doing them. Your church has special leaders, teachers, a pastor (some churches have several pastors), deacons and perhaps elders who will help you and teach you. You may be able to help boys and girls who are your age or younger.

Have tHESE LEaDERS at YOUR CHURCH SiGN tHEiR NaMES ON tHESE LiNES:

YOUR PaStOR _____

AN USHER _____

A BiBLE tEaCHER _____

BEING A MEMBER OF THE CHURCH MEANS THAT YOU SHOULD TRY TO MEET WITH YOUR CHURCH FAMILY OFTEN.

 The Bible says that people who are part of God's family "should not stay away from the church meetings, as some are doing." Hebrews 10:25

Being a member of the church means that you go there when you can (every Sunday, if possible). People are not just God's family on Sundays. They are God's people on Monday, Tuesday, Wednesday, Thursday, Friday and Saturday too. Followers of Jesus live in different places and speak different languages, but they all belong to God's family because they love Jesus and obey Him.

LIST TWO OCCASIONS WHEN PEOPLE AT YOUR CHURCH HAVE MEETINGS AND ACTIVITIES EACH WEEK:

1. _____

2. _____

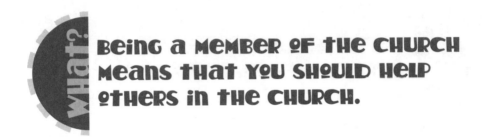

BEING A MEMBER OF THE CHURCH MEANS THAT YOU SHOULD HELP OTHERS IN THE CHURCH.

That's why Jesus told the people who followed Him to work together. When we work together Jesus can do His work through us. Remember, the church is God's family. It takes everyone working together for the job to be done. Doesn't it work best when everyone helps at your home?

IDEAS ON HOW TO HELP YOUR CHURCH FAMILY:

IDEA 1 Rory (age 7): "I help with the gardening at church."

IDEA 2 Seth (age 5): "After every church service, I empty the trash baskets."

IDEA 3 Eric (age 9): "I carried food with my mom to the Green family when they were sick."

IDEA 4 What is one idea you have to help?

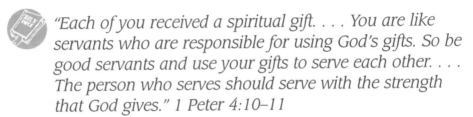

"Each of you received a spiritual gift. . . . You are like servants who are responsible for using God's gifts. So be good servants and use your gifts to serve each other. . . . The person who serves should serve with the strength that God gives." 1 Peter 4:10–11

WHO CAN JOIN A CHURCH?

 "But some people did accept him [Jesus]. They believed in him. To them he gave the right to become children of God." John 1:12

 "Then those people who accepted what Peter said were baptized. About 3,000 people were added to the number of believers that day." Acts 2:41

NUMBER THE EVENTS LISTED IN THE SECOND VERSE IN THE ORDER THAT THEY HAPPENED. *Put a number 1 by the first, a 2 by the second and a 3 by the third.*

 SOME BELIEVED IN JESUS AFTER HEARING PETER SPEAK.

 THESE PEOPLE WHO BELIEVED IN JESUS WERE BAPTIZED.

 THEY BECAME PART OF THE CHURCH.

Just as you must do certain things to join a team or group, there is one thing you must do before you join your church. You must be a member of God's family. The followers of Jesus in the Bible counted people as members of the church only after they became a part of God's family by accepting Jesus as their Savior.

MUST I BE A CERTAIN AGE BEFORE I CAN BE A PART OF THE CHURCH?

Your age is not important. You must be a part of God's family before you can be a part of the church.

A 10-YEAR-OLD BOY WHO IS PART OF GOD'S FAMILY IS A PART OF THE CHURCH.

A GIRL IN THE 12TH GRADE IN HIGH SCHOOL WHO IS NOT PART OF GOD'S FAMILY IS NOT A MEMBER OF THE CHURCH.

Question

ARE YOU PART OF GOD'S FAMILY?

IF YES, WHEN DID YOU DO THIS?

_____

IF NO, ARE YOU READY TO BECOME A PART OF GOD'S FAMILY NOW?

_____

You can decide right now to join God's family by praying like this:

DeaR JesUS,
THank YoU FoR LoVinG Me enoUGH to
Die on tHe CRoSS to PaY FoR MY Sin. I
KnoW I Do WRonG tHinGS. PLease
FoRGiVe Me FoR aLL tHe WRonG
tHinGS tHat I'Ve Done. I
Want YoU to CoMe into MY
LiFe. HeLP Me to CHooSe
to Do WHat YoU Want Me
to Do. THank YoU FoR
MaKinG Me YoUR CHiLD anD
a MeMBeR oF YoUR FaMiLY.
AMen.

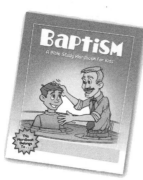

Baptism is a special way people show that Jesus is in their life and they are part of God's family. One way to learn more about baptism is to get the wordbook called *Baptism* in this series. See the back cover for ordering information.

HOW DO I JOIN MY CHURCH?

IF YOU ARE A PART OF GOD'S FAMILY, THEN YOU ARE A PART OF HIS CHURCH!

But you also attend a local church. Each local church is made up of people who love God and join together to worship each Sunday.

WHAT IS THE NAME OF YOUR LOCAL CHURCH? _____

YOU CAN BE A MEMBER OF YOUR LOCAL CHURCH WHEN YOU ARE OLDER.

Members of a local church are responsible for how the church runs. There may be a group of people who make the important decisions. Occasionally, there may be meetings that the members attend to make decisions.

If you want to be a member of your local church, you should talk to your pastor to find out how old you need to be to join your church and what other things you need to do to join.

Joining your local church is a decision only you can make. No one can choose for you. You should not do it just because someone encourages you. Instead, you should join because you want to be a part of your church and help in any way you can.

Remember, even if you are too young to join your local church, you are already a member of **THE CHURCH** if you've asked Jesus into your life.

WHAT HAVE YOU LEARNED ABOUT THE CHURCH?

GOOD REASON, WRONG REASON

Answer the questions as best you can without help from anyone else. **You may look back in the wordbook for answers.**

1. WHICH OF THE FOLLOWING REASONS DOES THE BIBLE SAY ARE GOOD REASONS FOR GOING TO CHURCH? *Place a check in the circle that is your answer.*

	GOOD Reason	WRONG Reason
TELLING JOKES	◯	◯
BEING A BULLY	◯	◯
WORSHIPING GOD	◯	◯
WEARING NEW CLOTHES	◯	◯
WANTING TO GO TO CHURCH	◯	◯

2. Write one thing that the Bible says people should do at church:

_____

3. Fill in the missing words:

"A church is a group of people who are members of God's family

and meet together to _____ and _____ what pleases Him."

TRUE/False

Write **T** for true or **F** for false in the space provided.

_____ **1.** Every member of God's family goes to heaven.

_____ **2.** A church is just a pretty building . . . nothing more.

_____ **3.** Joining your church is your decision.

_____ **4.** A church works best when everybody fights with one another and does what they want to do.

_____ **5.** Jesus works in people's hearts to make every church the way He wants it to be.

_____ **6.** The Bible says that it is good for members of God's family to go to church often and meet with other Christians.

_____ **7.** The Bible says that God has something special for you to do at the church where you attend.

_____ **8.** The Bible says that people should join a church even if they don't believe in Jesus.

Now Have a parent or teacher grade your quiz.